PAN AMERICAN FLIGHT #863
to Paradise!

From the author's small town of Panganiban to the vast plains of America, including collection of inspirational poems & other literary works.
(Sequel to the "The Thing of Beauty is a Joy Forever")

VOLUME I

FRANK A. DE LA ROSA

Copyright © Frank A. De La Rosa. All rights reserved.

No part of this publication may be reproduced, distributed, or transmitted in any form or by any means, including photocopying, recording, or other electronic or mechanical methods, without the prior written permission of the publisher, except in the case of brief quotations embodied in reviews and certain other non-commercial uses permitted by copyright law.

ISBN: 978-1-958895-34-4 (Hardback Edition)
ISBN: 978-1-958895-35-1 (E-book Edition)

Printed in the United States.

CONTENTS

Section	Pages
Dear Lord,	9
With God Nothing Is Impossible	18
Today	21
We Said A Prayer For You Today	24
A Gift That Costs Nothing	27
Live Up To Your Dreams!	32
Never Found The Time	35
Christmas Is Here Again With Us	38
You Can Make A Difference In Your World	41
A Tribute To: Maria Gracia Garcia De La Rosa	44
The Life Of A Caregiver By Frank A. De La Rosa	47
Bits & Pieces:	50
I've Learned...	53
Heavens Grocery Store	56
A Morning Prayer	60
Dad, A God's Masterpiece	63
Chunky Green Papaya Sauce	65
God Is Never Far Away	67
Give Me A Grateful Heart, Lord	70
God Will Take Care Of You	73
I Live Alone	76
Comes The Dawn	79
Some Golden Words To Live By	82
Coconut Oil The Healthiest Oil In The World	84
Catanduanes Beloved	85
Answered Prayer	86
A Gift That Cost Nothing	87

A Mother's Love ... 89
Alma Mater Song ... 90
A Child Learns ... 92
The Florence Nightingale Pledge ... 93
I Am Not There ... 94
Special Wishes For You ... 95
May The Good Lord Bless And Keep You ... 96
Let There Be Peace On Earth ... 97
Message ... 98
Footprints In The Sand ... 99
A Timeless Message Exerpted From Pope Francis In One Of His Homilies: ... 101
The Rose Within ... 102
How To Stay Young ... 103
Psalm 23 ... 104
A Psalm Of Life ... 105
Panaguican Hill ... 106
Philippine National Anthem ... 107
Pambansang Awit Ng Pilipinas ... 108
Bayan Ko ... 109
A Time For Everything... ... 110

Dear Lord,

Dear Lord, help me. For this day I go out into the world alone, and without your hand to guide me, I will wander far from the path which leads to success and happiness.

I ask not for gold or garment or even opportunities equal to my ability, instead guide me so that I may acquire ability equal to my opportunities.

Help me to remain patient through obstacles and failures, yet hide not from mine eyes the prize that will come with victory.

Assign me tasks to which others have failed; yet pluck the seeds of success from their failures. Confront me with fears that will temper my spirit; yet endow me with courage to face the challenges ahead of me.

Spare sufficient days to reach my goals; yet help me to live this day as though it be last.

Guide me in my words that they may bear fruit; yet silence my lips that none be maligned.

Discipline me in the habit of trying and trying again; yet show me the way to make use of the law of averages. Favor me with alertness to recognize opportunity; yet endow me with patience which will concentrate my strength.

Bathe me in good habits that the bad ones may drown; yet grant me compassion for weakness in others; suffer me to know that all things shall pass; yet help me to count my blessings of today.

Expose me to compassion and understanding, and fill my cup with love to turn strangers into friends.

But all these things be only if thy will. I am small and a lonely grape clutching the vine yet thou hast made me different from all others. Verily, there must be a special place for me. Guide me. Help me. Show me the way.

Let me become all you planned for me when my seed was planted and selected by you to sprout in the vineyard of the world.

So help me, God.

*T*his book is lovingly dedicated
to my eldest son, Dexter and his wife Katie and their 2 children
Caroline and Madeline and my eldest daughter Cindy, MD (Pediatrician).

Their mom, Demie, RN. Died October 2, 1978.

My eldest son, Dexter Francis De La Rosa.
(An Accountant & an MIS Financial Analyst).

Cindy G. De La Rosa (Pediatrician)

Doctor of Medicine, Manila, Philippines
Resident, Yale University @ Bridgeport Hospital, CT
Fellowship: University of Maryland Hospital, MD
Practicing Pediatrician in Philadelphia, USA

*The ROSE within each of us, nurtures it.
If you don't water your Rose in your garden, it will die.*

*Have a trip via Planet Earth @ EPCOT Center
@ Walt Disney World, Orlando Florida*

What a wonder can a beautiful light do to brighten your day!

Wow! The Banana Heart is Born. Puso ng Saging.

Frank Aggie Dela Rosa January 26, 2017 Hello kababayans! Please join us in our Heritage Festival at Our Lady of Grace Catholic Church, 300 Malabar Road SE, Palm Bay, Florida 32907, from January 27, 28 & 29 this weekend. It would be nice if you could come on Sunday, the 29th at 10:30AM for the Heritage Festival Mass, Parade of Nations, followed by Taste of Grace, the food of all Nations.

The Golden Grain in America!

Super hot Labuyo pepper.

All things bright and beautiful...

*A beautiful rose blooms at my garden gate.
Freshly taken with my tiny winnie digital camera.*

The beautiful Rose blooming at my garden gate.

WITH GOD NOTHING IS IMPOSSIBLE

There is no difficulty that God cannot conquer,

No disease that God cannot heal,

No door that God cannot open,

No gulf that God cannot bridge,

No wall that God cannot throw down,

No sin that God cannot redeem,

Because with God nothing is impossible.

It makes no difference how deeply seated the problem,

How hopeless the outlook,

How muddled the the tangle,

How great the mistake,

A sufficient rrealization of forgiving and forgetting will disolve it all...

If only you can forgive enough and forget enough...

You would be the happiest person in the world,

Because with God nothing is impossible to accomplish.

-Emmet Fox

The Dogwood tree in my yard in the Winter. I just loved playing with colors and harmony in my PC. This is one of the beauties of Winter. After the Winter comes the Spring!

My beautiful Magnolia flower in my yard.

The colors of Spring!

TODAY

I may never see tomorrow
There is no written guarantee
And the things that happened yesterday
Belong to history.

I cannot predict the future
I cannot change the past
I just have the present moment
I must treat it as my last.

I must use this moment wisely
For it soon will pass away.
And be lost to me forever
As part of yesterday.

I must exercise compassion
Help the fallen to their feet
Be a friend unto the friendless
Make an empty life complete.

The unkind things I do today
May never be undone
And the friendship that I have failed to win
May never be won.

I may never have another chance
On bended knee to pray
Thank God with humble heart
For giving me TODAY.

A 5-lb Pomelo Fruit. Just so large & heavy!

Playing with colors with a new bloom of Hybrid Hibiscus in my garden. Hibiscus on BLUE.

You can see the face of God in every flower (Plumeria/calachuichi).

The whole new dimension of a Giant Ripe Pomelo.

We Said A Prayer For You Today

To: All our FB Friends

We said a prayer for you today
And know God must have heard...
We felt the answer in our hearts
Although He spoke no word.
We didn't ask for wealth or fame
We knew you wouldn't mind
We asked Him to send treasures
Of a far lasting kind.

We asked that He'd be near you
At the start of each new day
To grant you health and blessings
And friends to share your way.

We asked for happiness for you
In all things great and small...
But it was for His loving care
We prayed the most of all.

Love & Prayer,
My Mary Grace and Me

A new bloom of Samapaguita (Kampupot) multipetaled variety.

An imaginative Roadway to Heaven!

*This is the mural that I found in one of my rooms.
I just loved to share it with you.*

So beautiful to greet me. My beautiful Pink Plumeria.

A GIFT THAT COSTS NOTHING

A smile costs nothing, but gives much. It enriches those who receive, without making poorer those who give. It takes but a moment, but the memory of it sometimes last forever. None is so rich or mighty that he can get along without it, and none is so poor that he cannot be rich by it. A smile creates happiness in the home, fosters good will in business, and is the countersign of friendship. It brings rest to the weary, and cheer to the discouraged, sunshine to the sad, and it is a nature's best antidote for trouble. Yet it cannot be bought, begged, borrowed, or stolen, for it is something that is of no value to anyone until it given away. Some people are too tired to give you a smile. Give them one of yours, as none needs a smile so much as he who has no more to give.

The use of Solar Energy! The whole world has to know that I'm cooking my food in my SOLAR OVEN right now. No stirring! No watching! No burning! And the food is naturally delicious from its own juice.

The City of Melbourne in the background.

Good news again! Showing my freshly cooked pork chops in my new Solar Oven. So juicy and tender. Just specially delicious. I just loved my new Solar Oven. No need to watch. No need to stir. Won't get burn... because the heat is evenly distributed all around the pot.

From Yours Truly... Advance Message of Thanks to all my FB friends. Here's yours truly sending you his message of thanks and goodwill. Yes, my dear friends, I cannot seem to describe this moment and every moment as my special day approaches. I have seen your "likes". Behind those "likes" I have seen your smiles and shining faces.

The other mural that I found in my other room. I just loved the graphics.

My favorite water plant in the house. It gives me so much Oxygen at night while I'm aslept.

My garden as viewed from my new porch, I watched them yesterday dancing in the rain.

The only bunch in the grapevine. Is it sweet?

Live Up To Your Dreams!

*D*on't underestimate your worth by comparing yourself with others. It is because we are different; each of us is special. Don't set your goals by what other people deem important. Only you know what is best for you. Don't take for granted the things closest to your heart. Cling to them as you would your life, for without them, life is meaningless. Don't let your life slip through your fingers by living in the past or for the future. By living your life one day at a time, you will live all the days of your life. Don't give up when you still have something to give. Nothing is really over until the moment you stop trying.

Don't be afraid to encounter risks. It is by taking chances that we learn how to be brave. The quickest way to receive love is to give love; the fastest way to lose love is to hold it too tightly, and the best way to keep love is to give it wings. Don't give up your dreams; to be without dreams is to be without hope; to be without hope is to be without purpose. Don't run through life too fast that you forget not only where you've been, but also where you are going. Life is not a race, but a journey to be savored each and every step of the way. Life is beautiful, enjoy it! Life is a song, sing it! Life is a dream, dream it. And above all, life is a gift from God, a gift so precious in His sight. We can never thank Him enough for this!

My flowering creep myrtle by the garden gate.

My garden in the rain. Dancing with joy.

My Golden Rain Tree is ready to bloom in our front yard.

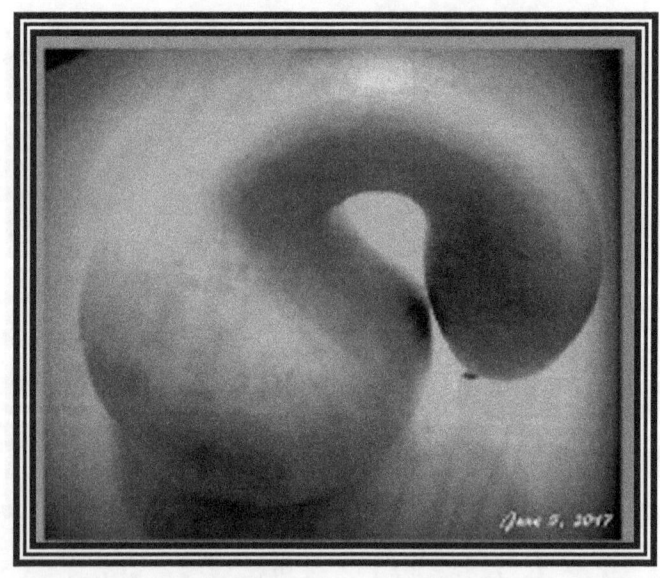

A Natural Work of Art by Paco of Florida. That's the fruit of my labor in my garden.

Never Found The Time

I knelt to pray but not for long,
I had too much to do.
I had to hurry and got to work,
For bills would soon be due.
So I knelt and said a hurried prayer,
And jumped off my knees.
My Christian duty was done,
My soul could now rest at ease.
All day long I had no time,
To spread a word of cheer.
No time to speak of Christ to friends,
They'd laugh at me I'd fear.
No time, no time, too much to do,
That was my constant cry.
No time to give to souls in need,
But at last the time has come... the time to die.
I went before the Lord,
I stood before Him with downcast eyes.
In His hands held a book,
It was the "Book of Life."
The Lord looked into His book and said,
"Your name I cannot find. I once was to
write it down...but never found the time."

**"Yes, indeed, there's no time for anything.
If you want time, find it!"**

My kale greens are abandoned. Anybody wants me?

The only boy De La Rosa of my eight grandchildren

CHRISTMAS IS HERE AGAIN WITH US

Christmas is here again with us. Christmas time is not only for gift-giving and parties. Christmas time is the best and special time to reflect on the birth of Jesus in the manger in Bethlehem that cold winter night when Mary and Joseph didn't find any room in the inn.

The birth of Jesus is the most special gift God, The Father has given us. It's His perfect present to the world through Our Virgin Mother Mary and her chased spouse Joseph. Jesus came into this world as a human person in the essence that He could feel what a human being really feels. But the truth is that God, The Father sent Jesus, to let the whole world knows and believes that there is God, the Creator of the human race. And that God lives within each of us. Jesus came to the world to live with us, to suffer with us, and to die with us. However, the greatest promise made by God, The Father to all of us, that Jesus was sent down to earth, to redeem us from sins and have ever lasting life. So, this Christmas, let's keep this in our hearts, that what we are is God's gift to us, and what we have is our gift to God. Let's all celebrate Christmas with joy for the coming of the Messiah in the person of Baby Jesus in the manger. Alleluia! Alleluia! This is the day the Lord has made, let's all rejoice and be glad in it. Alleluia!

My favorite garden corner patch.

This season bountiful harvest. So fresh! So tender! So organic!

My green tomatoes showing off her beauty.

Alumanda flowering bush.

YOU CAN MAKE A DIFFERENCE IN YOUR WORLD

It's not how much you accomplish in life
that really matters,
but how much you give to others.
It's not how high you build your dreams
that makes a difference,
but how high your faith can climb.
It's not how many goals you reach,
but how many lives you touch.
It's not who you know that matters,
but who you are inside.
Believe in the impossible,
hold tight to the incredible,
and live each day to its fullest potential.
You can make a difference in your world.

My gabbie garden patch.

My Gumamela flowering bush by the front entrance.

My High-Towering Christmas Tree in the front yard.

Fireburst bush with red tiny flowers.

A Tribute to:
MARIA GRACIA GARCIA DE LA ROSA
Born: October 2, 1942; Died: March 30, 2016

*Y*our gentle face
And pleasant smile
With heavenly peace we recall
You had a kindly word for each
And died beloved by all.
The voice is mute
And still the heart
That loved us well and true.
Oh, bitter was the trial to part
From one so good and loving as you.
You are not forgotten, my darling dear
Nor will you ever be
As long as life and memory last
We will remember you.
We miss you now
Our hearts are sore
As time goes by
We miss you more and more.
Your loving smile
Your gentle face
No one can fill your place.

-From Loving Husband & Family

My beefsteak green tomatoes.

Always so proud of my garden!

My Sweet Potato Patch.

Frank among his creep myrtle flowers by the driveway.

THE LIFE OF A CAREGIVER

by Frank A. De La Rosa

The life of a caregiver is a commitment
Twenty-four hour 'round the clock, tic-tac
It's a 24/7 job, while others have only eight
All through the night and day, I'm by the patient's side.

The days are short and the nights are long
The CNA and the nurse come along...
The needs of the patient are plenty during the day
And at the nighttime it's only my patient and me.

The morning comes
The blood glucose reading is due
I have to look for the strips and the lancets
Only to find out that the glucose meter's batteries are low.

The blood glucose reading is high
She needs an insulin shot
Following a sliding scale
Using the syringe I took 10 units to complete the shot.

The medications are to be given at different times Some are 6:00AM; some are 9:00; some are in the evening There are so much to remember, and a lot of concentrations To give all these medications.

Still, I have to prepare the meals
The breakfast, the lunch and the supper
What do I have to cook
When I don't know even how to follow the recipe book.

I did my best to prepare all the meals
With so much veggies from our garden
My cooking comes out so delicious and nutritious
Only to know that my patient, my beloved wife, is getting strong.

Bunga ng Condol. Kay laki na!
(The fruit of a Winter melon is getting bigger)

Magnolia flower.

A rose by any other name is as sweet.
(William Shakespeare)

BITS & PIECES:

*I*f God for a second, forgot what I have become and granted me, a little bit to the best of my ability, I wouldn't possibly say everything that is in my mind, but I would be more thoughtful of all I say.

I would give merit to things not for what they are worth, but for what they meant to express. I would sleep little, I would dream more, because I know that every minute we close our eyes, we waste 60 seconds of light. I would walk while others stop. I would awake while others sleep.

If God would give me a little bit more of life, I would dress in a simple manner. I would place myself in front of the sun, leaving not only my body, but my soul naked at its mercy. To the older ones, I would say how mistaken they are when they think they stop falling in love when they grow old, without knowing that they grow old only when they stop falling in love.

I would give wings to children, but I would leave it to them how to fly by themselves. To the elderly, I would say that death doesn't arrive when they grow old, but with forgetfulness.

I have learned so much with all the people I met along life's journey. I have learned that everybody wants to live on top of the mountain, without knowing that true happiness is obtained in the journey taken and the form used to reach the top of the hill. I have learned that when a newborn baby holds, with its little hand, his father's finger, it has trapped him for the rest of his life. I have learned that a man has the right and obligation to look down at another man, only when that man needs help to get up from the ground.

Say always what you feel, not what you think. If I knew that today is the last time I saw you, I would hug you, with all my strength and I would pray to the Lord to let me the guardian angel of your soul. If I knew these are the last moments to see you, I would say "I love you". There is always tomorrow, and life gives us another opportunity to do things right, but in case I am wrong, and today is all that is left to me, I would love to tell you how much I love you and that I will never forget you.

Tomorrow is never guaranteed to anyone, young or old. Today could be the last time to see your loved ones, which is why you must not wait, do it today, in case tomorrow never arrives. I am sure you will be sorry you wasted the opportunity today to give a smile, a hug, a kiss, and that you were too busy to grant them their

last wish.

Hanging in the tree is my Green Sugar Apple (Atis). Ready to pick by September.

My Condol fruit is getting so huge! The pull of Gravity makes it so.

Baby Jesus found a beautiful home! Baby Jesus & Me. Baby Jesus, please keep me safe, my family & friends.

I just bought a cactus plant for a birthday gift. I hoped that she'll like it. Very easy to maintain. Do you like it too? Comments please. Thanks!

I've Learned...

I've learned that, no matter what happens how bad it seems today, life does go on, and it will be better tomorrow.

I've learned that you can tell a lot about a person by the way he/she handles three things: a rainy day, lost luggage, and a tangled Christmas tree lights.

I've learned that, regardless of your relationship with your parents, you'll miss them when they're gone from your life.

I've learned that making a "living" is not the same thing as making a "life".

I've learned that life sometimes gives you a second chance. I've learned that you shouldn't go through life with a catcher's mitt on both hands. You need to be able to throw something back.

I've learned that if you pursue happiness, it will elude you. But, if you focus on your family, your friends, the needs of others, your work and doing the very best you can, happiness will find you.

I've learned that whatever I decide something with an open heart, I usually make the right decision.

I've learned that every day, you should reach out and touch someone; people love a human touch - holding hands, a warm hug, or just a friendly pat on the back.

Sometimes people just need a little something to make them smile. People will forget what you said, people will forget what you did ... but people will never forget how you made them feel.

I've learned ... that I still have a lot to learn...

*This was the church (rebuilt) where I was baptized and confirmed..way back before WW II.
In my beautiful hometown of Panganiban, Catanduanes, Philippines.
Photo courtesy: Bryan del Sur*

My Banana and Papaya Corner.

My Seniguelas Fruit Trees so green & lush!

My Magnolia flower getting ready to open.

Heavens Grocery Store

As I was walking down life's highway many years ago
I came upon a sign that read Heavens Grocery Store.

When I got a little closer the doors swung open wide
And when I came to myself I was standing inside.

I saw host of angels. They were standing everywhere.
One handed me a basket and said, "My child shop with care."

Everything a human needed was in that grocery store.
And what you could not carry you could come back for more.

First I got some Patience. Love was in that same row.
Further down was Understanding, you needed that wherever you go.

I got a box or two of Wisdom and Faith a bag or two.
And Charity of course, I need some of that too.

I couldn't miss the Holy Ghost, it was all over the place.
And some Strength and Courage, to help me run the race.

My basket was getting full but I remembered I needed Grace.
And I then I chose Salvation for Salvation was for free.
I tried to get enough of that to do for for you and me.

Then I went to the counter to pay for my grocery bill,
For I thought I had everything to do the Master's will.

As I went up to the aisle I saw Prayer and put that in,
For I know when I stepped outside I would run into sin.

Peace and Joy were plentiful, the last thing on the shelf.
Song and Praise were hanging near so I just helped myself.

Then I said to the angel, "Now how much I owe you?"
He smiled and said, "Just take them everywhere you go.
"Again I asked, "Really now, how much do I owe?"
"My child", he said, "God paid your bill a long time ago."

The whole world of flowers!

The Floating Garden @ WDW...EPCOT Center, Orlando Florida.

The Pride of the Bicol Region, the majestic Mt. Mayon!

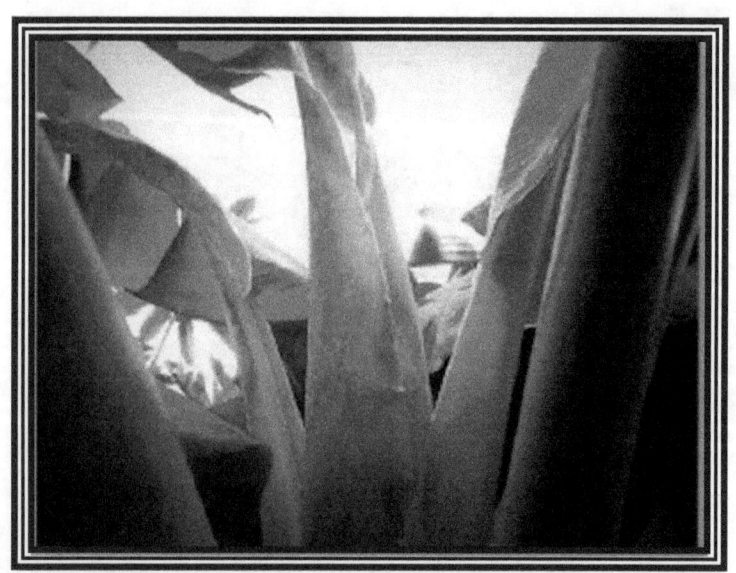

News for today: My dwarf SABA is delivering her 1st Baby Heart. (Haha...Puso ng Saging).

O. Virgin Mother from thy throne, so bright and bliss above, protect thy child and cheer my path, with thy sweet smile of love. Mother dear, remember me, and never cease thy care; till in heaven eternally, thy love and bliss I share.

God always wanted us to be HAPPY!

A Morning Prayer

This morning when I wakened
and saw the sun above,
I softly said, "Good morning, Lord,
bless our families, friends & relatives,
far and near."
Right away, I thought of you
And said a loving prayer,
That God would bless you specially,
And keep you away from care.
I thought of all the God's blessings for you
A day could hold in store,
I wished it all for you
Because no one deserves it more.
This is a thoughtful prayer
To show you that care.
Love always grows
When we generously share.
May God graciously bless you
And keep you in His loving care
Today, tomorrow, and always.

This is an adventure in Photography.
Playing with Self-Portrait with my tiny winnie digital camera.

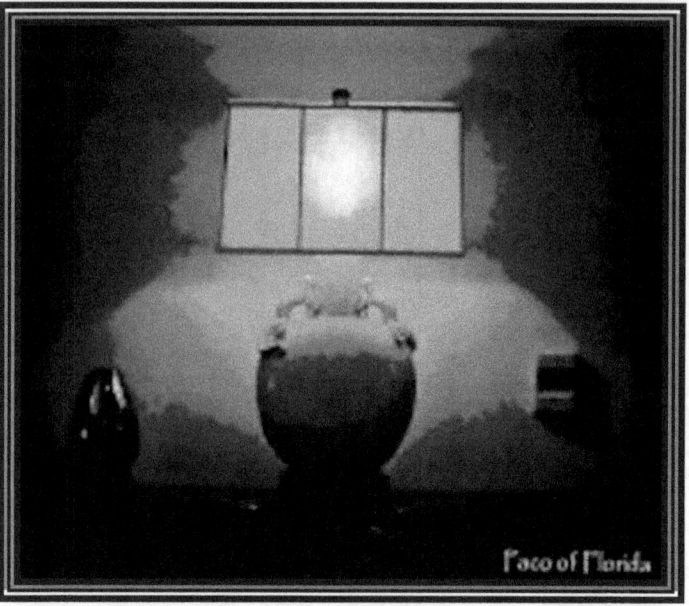

Creating a simple work of art in a lampshade.

Down Memory Lane.

Dad, A God's Masterpiece

God took the strength of a mountain,
The majesty of a tree,
The warmth of a summer sun,
The calm of a quiet sea,
The generous soul of nature,
The comforting arm of night,
The wisdom of the ages,
The power of the eagle's flight,
The joy of the morning in spring,
The faith of a mustard seed,
The patience of eternity, The
depth of a family need, Then
combined these qualities,
When there was nothing more to add,
He knew His masterpiece complete,
And so He called it Dad.

Haha...I am watching my Dwarf Saba delivers her First Baby Heart. Puso ng Saging.

The Lemon Grass in all its beauty!

Chunky Green Papaya Sauce

Ingredients:

4lbs. green papayas, cored and cut in chunks
(about 2 large fruits)
1 cup water
½ cup brown sugar
Thai Basil
Lemon Grass kitchen string

Procedure:

In 8-quart Dutch oven combine papayas, Thai basil or lemon grass and one cup of water. Bring to a boil, then reduce heat. Simmer, covered, for 20 minutes or until papayas are soft. Remove basil or lemon grass. Mash papayas with large spoon or potato masher. Sweeten to taste with granulated brown sugar. Stir before serving. Put in jars. Last up to 3 weeks in the refrigerator or 6 months in freezer.

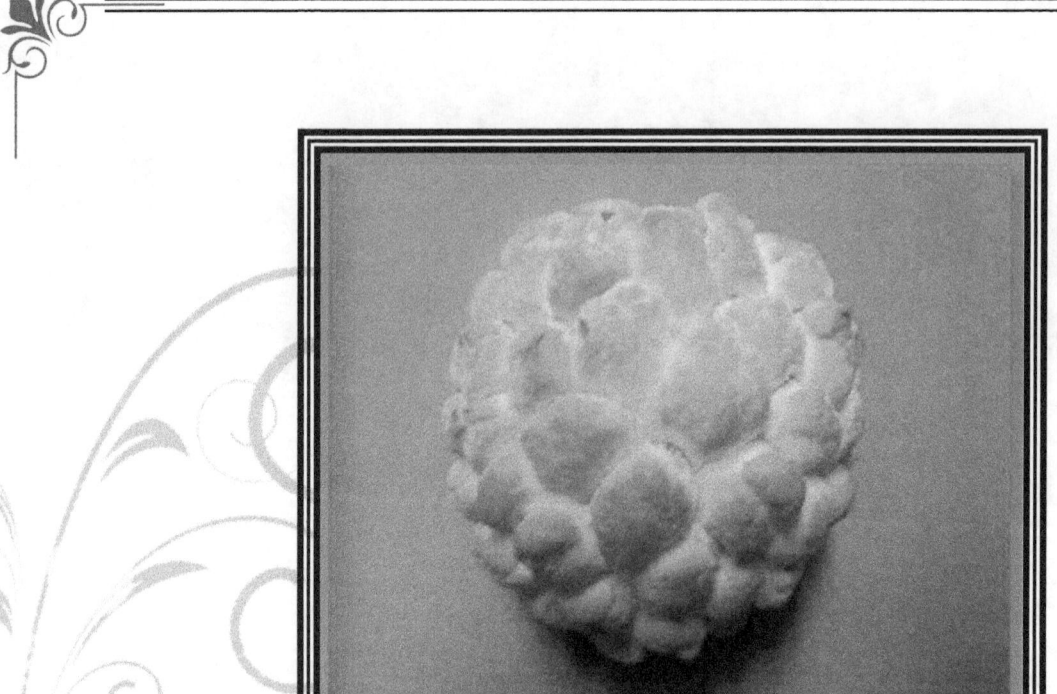

Ripe Sugar Apple (Atis).

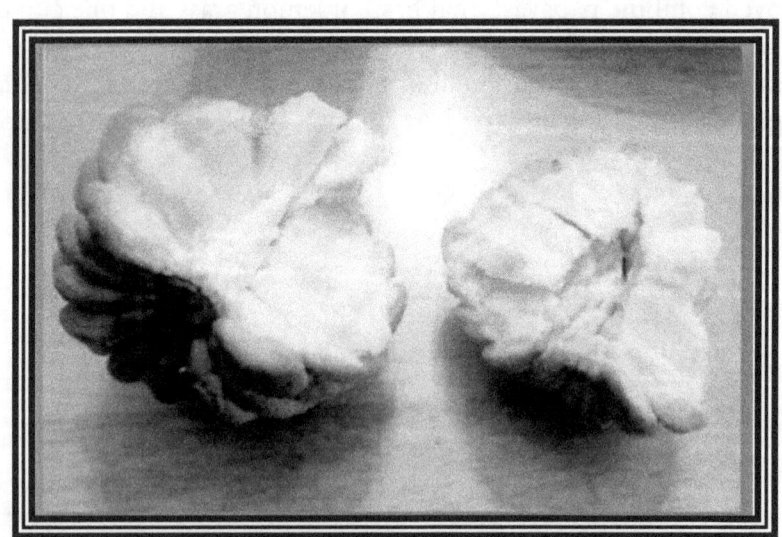

Divided ripe Atis.

God Is Never Far Away

*G*od isn't far away;
He surrounds you with His love.
It was He who opened
your eyes this morning.
It is His strength that will carry
you through this day,
and it is in His peace
that your heart will
find rest tonight.
God isn't far away.
He is the light of this day.
He is the sky above you,
And the earth beneath you,
And the life of every living thing.
He is in every smile,
In every thought that gives you hope,
In every tear that waters your soul,
And every moment you can't face alone.
He's the love on your loved one's face.
He's in friends along the way-
In strangers you have yet to meet,
And blessings you have yet to receive.
He's in every good thing that touches you.
He is in every step you make,
And every breath you take.
God is not far away,
For He is with you always.

One summer morning in my yard.

I always kept my mind open, on how I can make a simple work of art, out of my garden produce. Here is just a sample from my giant squash.

The JFK Rose.

The beautiful city of San Francisco in the golden state of California.

Give Me A Grateful Heart, Lord

Give me a grateful heart, Lord,
For each precious gift received.
As years unfold, may I behold
Life, still, through eyes enchanted.
Let me find beauty in all things,
Not be too blind to see
The goodness in my fellowmen,
That he would find in me.

Grant that my ears remain attuned
To hear the smallest sigh,
And may I lend a gentle touch,
To less sure than I.
Let me remember lessons learned,
To profit from the past,
And may I build a bridge of dreams,
That shall forever last.

Let me rejoice in simple things;
I need no wealth to buy
The scent of pine upon the wind,
A burnished copper sky,
Scarlet roses on the fence,
Sunrise through the trees —
Oh, gran that I may not outgrow
Affinity of these!

Give me a grateful heart, Lord;
Let me be satisfied
When days are less sunny
And plan lie at low tide.
Life is a sweet adventure
That will lead to who know where,
So, give me a grateful heart, Lord,
That You will always be near..

Hurricane Maria, please stay in the ocean where you belong. My Papaya Tree is not that strong to withstand you.

FB: Celebrate International Day of Peace with this frame on your profile picture.

After the storm comes the calm.

My Pandan plant...so healthy and so fresh!

God Will Take Care of You

*M*ay your heart always find peace
and comfort in the knowledge that
you are never alone.
May God's presence ease your spirit
and give you rest when you need it.
He knows how you feel.
He is ever aware of your circumstances
and ready to be your strength, your courage,
and your peace.
He is there to cast sunlight when your
days are low; to send encouragement
through the love of friends and family,
and to replace your weariness with new hope.
God is your stronghold, and with Him as
your guide, you need never be afraid. No
circumstances can block His love. No
pain is too hard for Him to bear.
No task is too difficult for Him to complete.
What you are experiencing is simply too deep
for words. God understands.
He is your Strength -
today, tomorrow, and always.
And He loves you very much.
Cast all your cares in Him -
And everything will come smoothly
in place! We'll keep you in our prayers.

*This is my multi-colored PUMPKIN for THANKSGIVING!
Anyone wants a slice after Thanksgiving to bake into a pie?*

Friends are the ROSES in life's bouquet..

A beautiful Banana Heart was born! Puso ng Sagging.

God never allows a burden heavier than we can carry. No matter what, He wants us to be happier than sad. If birds sing after a storm, why can't we? No one has travelled the bridge of success without ever crossing the streets of trials. God never promised us an easy journey in life, only safety on board…Smile, then be happy! If you travel with God, you can be sure how the journey is going to end. God bless you more than you can imagine…

Prayer is the greatest gift that we can give away to anyone, at anytime, and at any place.

I Live Alone

I live alone, dear Lord,
Stay by my side,
In all my daily needs
Be Thou my guide.
Grant me good health,
For that indeed, I pray,
To carry on my work
From day to day.
Keep pure my mind,
My thoughts, my every deed,
Let me be kind, unselfish
In my neighbor's need. Spare
me from fire, from flood From
malicious tongues.
From thieves, from fear,
And evil ones.
If sickness or an accident befall,
Then humbly, Lord I pray,
Hear Thou my call,
And when I'm feeling low,
Or in despair,
Lift up my heart
And help me in my prayer.
I live alone, dear Lord,
Yet I have no fear,
Because I feel your Presence
Ever near.

The dad of Cindy, Dexter, Joy and Francis.

Yellow Chayote in my garden. So delicious!

*Frank doing **Fall** gardening.*

Comes The Dawn

*After a while you learn the subtle difference between holding a
hand and chaining a soul.*

*And you learn that love doesn't mean leaning and company
doesn't mean security, and you begin to understand that kisses
are not contracts and presents aren't promises,
and you begin to accept your defeats with your head up high and
your eyes open, with the grace of a woman not a grief of a child.*

*You learn to build your roads on today because tomorrow's
ground is too uncertain for plans, and futures have a way of
falling down in mid-flight.*

After a while you learn that even sunshine burns if you get too much.

*So plant your own garden and decorate
your own soul, instead of waiting for someone to bring you flowers.*

*And learn that you really can endure, that you really are strong,
and you really have worth, you learn and learn ...
with every goodbye you learn.*

Hoho....a memory of Christmas past.

Green...green...my garden covers of green.

*A life-size Philippine Parol. Home-made by Frank.
Located on the over-hung of our front door.*

Light makes everything beautiful.

Some Golden Words to Live by...

*C*ount your years
by the flowers that you grow,
never by the leaves that fall.

Count your days by the happy moments,
don't remember your cares at all.

Count your night by stars,
not shadows when the evening falls.

Count your moments with smiles and laughter,
not tears and sorrows.

Count your blessings,
not aches or pains, or disappointments.

Count your age by rainbows,
Not number of passing clouds at all.

May your life be filled with flowers,
friends, smiles, and laughter.

Add life to your years;
not years to your life,
for life is meant for living and to be enjoyed!

Remember that: When life hands you lemons, make
lemonade. And share it with everyone! Smile!

HAPPY DAYS ARE HERE TO STAY!

My beautiful Magnolia flower.

A True Florida Color!

Coconut Oil
The Healthiest Oil in the World

Uses:

a. Reduces risk of atherosclerosis and related illness
b. Reduces risk of cancer and other degenerative conditions.
c. Help prevent, bacterial, viral and fungal (including yeast) infections.
d. Supports immune system functions.
e. Helps prevent osteoporosis.
f. Helps control diabetes.
g. Promotes weight loss.
h. Supports healthy metabolic function.
1. Provides an immediate source of energy.
J. Supplies fewer calories than other fats.
k. Supplies important nutrients necessary for good health.
1. Improves digestion and nutrient absorption.
m. Has a mild delicate flavor.
n. Is highly resistant to spoilage (long shelf life).
o. Is heat resistant (the healthiest oil for cooking).
p. Helps skin soft and smooth.
q. Helps prevent premature aging and wrinkling of the skin.
r. Helps protect against skin cancer and other blemishes.

As unbelievable as it sounds, the oil in coconuts has been found to aid the body in destroying dozens of harmful viruses including hepatitis C, herpes, and HIV. Coconut oil has been called the healthiest dietary oil on earth. If you are not using coconut oil for your daily cooking and body care needs, you are missing out on one of nature's most amazing health products. In using coconut oil, you will discover other healing miracles. Each health benefit is explained and fully documented by scientific research by Dr. Bruce Fife. Dr. Fife is commended for bringing together this breakthrough in the positive benefits of coconut oil. With his book on the subject, the inquiring reader will have a new and balanced view of the role of fat and specially saturated fats in our diet. Look for an extra virgin coconut oil which is available in natural food store in your neighborhood.

CATANDUANES BELOVED

*I*sle of the Eastern Seas
Where the morning sunbeams creeping on the trees
Land of the sun-caressed
So free and so lovingly sweet
Home sweet home
Under the summer skies
Where the fragrant roses
Blooming on the vales
Refrain:
Dear Catanduanes
bring me back to thee
Home of joy and people free.
Come now , O, Come
My love to Catanduanes our home
Calling bitter life to pleasure and ease
With a love so true and tenderly sweet

(Yes my love)
Yonder our way
The trail to the land of the sun-caressed
Dear Catanduanes bring me back to thee
Home of joy and people free.

Answered Prayer

I asked for Strength...
And God gave me Difficulties to make me strong;

I asked for Wisdom...
And God gave me Problems to solve;

I asked for Posterity...
And God gave me Brain and Brawn to work;

I asked for courage...
And God gave me Danger to overcome;

I asked for Love...
And God gave me troubled people to help;

I asked for Favors...
And God gave me Opportunities.

I received nothing I wanted...I received everything I needed.
I am among men richly blessed.

A GIFT THAT COST NOTHING

A smile cost nothing, but gives much. It enriches those who receive, without making poorer those who give. It takes but a moment, but the memory of it sometimes last forever. None is so rich or mighty that he can get along without it, and none is so poor that he cannot be rich by it. A smile creates happiness in the home, fosters good will in business, and is the countersign of friendship. It brings rest to the weary, and cheer to the discouraged, sunshine to the sad, and it is a nature's best antidote for trouble. Yet it cannot be bought, begged, borrowed, or stolen, for it is something that is of no value to anyone until it given away. Some people are too tired to give you a smile. Give them one of yours, as none needs a smile so much as he who has no more to give. The more you gave away...the happier this world would be..

Cyn & Dex with their grandma Natalie

Introducing Joy, my youngest daughter of Demie & I.

A Mother's Love

A Mother's love is something
that no one can explain,
It is made of deep devotion
and of sacrifice and pain,
It is endless and unselfish
and enduring come what may,
For nothing can destroy it
or take that love away... It is
patient and forgiving and all
others are forsaking,
And it never fails or falters
even though the heart is breaking...
It believes beyond believing
when the world around seems condemning,
And it glows with all the beauty
of the rarest brightest gems...
It is far beyond defining,
it defies all explanation,
And it still remains a secret
like the mysteries of creation...
A many, splendored miracle
man cannot understand,
And another wondrous evidence
of God's tender guiding hand.

Alma Mater Song

*L*oyal schoolmates come together
Be glad and let us sing
Give praise to Alma Mater
And let her glories ring
Let our duties noble and loving
For her bring honor high
For her our school inspiring
Our love shall never die
Long live Alma Mater's glory
Whose spirit shall guide us ever
With labor and faith and nobly
And dedication to her
Long life! Long live!
Alma Mater.

Sang during our Golden Jubilee Celebration
CALC Class '58 Reunion
Panganiban, Catanduanes

Flushing, New York - 1973

Frank and Demie at the wedding of Dr. Toti P. Gonzalo & Lucille La Penne, RN

A Child Learns

If a child lives with criticism,
He learns to condemn.

If a child lives with hostility,
He learns to fight.

If a child lives with fear,
He learns to be apprehensive.

If a child lives with pity,
He learns to be sorry for himself.

If a child lives with ridicule,
He learns to be shy.

If a child lives with jealousy,
He learns to entrust others.

If a child lives with shame,
He learns to feel guilty.

If a child lives with encouragement,
He learns to feel confident.

If a child lives with tolerance,
He learns to be appreciative.
If a child lives with acceptance,
He learns to love.

If a child lives with approval,
He learns to like himself.

If a child lives with recognition,
He learns that it is good to have a goal.

If a child lives with sharing,
He learns to be generous.

If a child lives with security,
He learns to have faith in
himself and others.

If a child lives with friendliness,
He learns that the world is a
place in which to live.

If you live with serenity,
Your child will live with peace of mind.

The Florence Nightingale Pledge

I solemnly pledge before God
And in the presence of this assembly,
To pass my life in purity
And to practice my profession faithfully,
I will abstain from whatever is deleterious
And mischievous,
And will not take or knowingly administer
Any harmful drug.
I will do all in my power to maintain
And elevate the standard of my profession, And
will hold in confidence all personal matters
Committed to my keeping and all family affairs
Coming to my knowledge
In the practice of my calling. With
loyalty will I endeavor to aid The
physician in his work,
And devote myself to the welfare
Of those committed to my care.
So help me God.

(I AM A NURSE)

I AM NOT THERE

Do not stand at my grave and weep:
I am not there. I do not sleep.
I am a thousand winds that blow.
I am the diamond glints on snow.
I am the sunlight on ripened grain.
I am the gentle autumn's rain.
When you awaken in the morning's hush,
I am the swift uplifting rush
Of quiet bird in circled flight.
I am the soft stars that shine at night.
Do not stand at my grave and cry:
I do not sleep,
I did not die.

A LOVING TRIBUTE TO:

To all our beloved departed classmates
CAlC Class '58.

SPECIAL WISHES FOR YOU

May God open up the windows of Heaven
and pour out the blessings...
you'll not have enough room
to receive them.

May God bless you
exceeding abundantly -
above all you could hope for.

And may God bless you -
that you may walk
in a financial overflow
for all the years to come.

We ask all these
In the name of our Lord,
Jesus Christ,
to whom all good things come.
Amen.

MAY THE GOOD LORD BLESS AND KEEP YOU

May the good Lord bless and keep you
Whether near or far away May
you find that long awaited
Golden day, today.

May your troubles all be small ones
And your fortune ten times ten May
the good Lord bless and keep you
Till we meet again.

May you walk with sunlight shining
And a blue bird in every tree
May there be a silver lining
Back of every cloud you see.

Fill your dreams with sweet tomorrows
Never mind what might have been
May the good Lord bless and keep you
Till we meet again...

LET THERE BE PEACE ON EARTH

Let there be peace on earth
And let it begin with me
Let there be peace on earth
The peace that was meant to be
With God as our Father
Families all are we
Let me walk with my brother
In perfect harmony
Let peace begin with me And
this be the moment now
With every step I take
Let this be my solemn vow
To take each moment
And live each moment eternally
In peace eternally
Let there peace on earth
And let it begin with me.

San Vicente Street
Panganiban, Catanduanes

MESSAGE

To Members of Class '58:

My warmest greetings to the members of Class '58, especially to the officers, and the surviving members of the Alicia Agricultural and Fishery School (now CAIC), who will be celebrating their Golden Jubilee Reunion on March 23, 24, & 25, 2008.

Your celebration as highlighted by the theme, "Yesterday's Fond Memories Will Be Remembered Today, Tomorrow, and Forever. ..", Demonstrates the noble mission of togetherness, closeness, and love among the graduates of Class '58. I, myself, and my family, welcome and enjoin each and everyone in this magnificent occasion. Let us brighten our awareness and continue in our commitment in our development efforts for the improvement our of Alma Mater.

Fifty years have passed, and if we have to look at each other, so many changes have taken place, like our faces, hair, voices, the way we walk, talk and sing, and almost everything. Anyway, this is a part of our lives. We just have to accept things as they come gracefully and tenderly.

Finally, let us march onward, welcome the challenges in life, and may God give us a longer life for us, to be able serve Him.

Good luck to one and all! And may the Good Lord bless us all.

(Sgd.) Mrs. Gertrudes A. Fernandez
Mentor, CAIC

Footprints in the Sand

One night I dreamed I was walking along the beach with the Lord
Scenes from my life flashed across the sky,
In each, I noticed footprints in the sand.
Sometimes there were two sets of footprints;
other times there was only one.

During the lowest times of my life
I could see only one set of footprints,
so I said, "Lord, you promised me,
that you would walk with me always.
Why, when I have needed you most would you leave me?"

The Lord replied, "My precious child,
I love you and would never leave you.
The times when you have seen only one set of footprints,
it was then that I carried you."

549 Andrew Street SE
Palm Bay, FL 32909
March 15, 2007

Mr. Larry Hellman, Fire Chief
Fire Prevention Bureau
5240 Babcock Street NE
Palm Bay, Florida 32905

Re: Brush Fires of March 2, 2007,
Andrew St. SE, Palm Bay, FL

Dear Fire Rescuers of Palm Bay:

I found an opportune time to write you today. What a scary afternoon on March 2, 2007. Our neighborhood was on fire!

My wife and I were on our way to attend the Good Friday late afternoon Mass at Our Lady of Grace Catholic Church in Palm Bay. As we started to drive on Andrew Street, where we live, we saw a smoke at a distance. Suddenly we saw a fire starting at the end of Andrew St. Within seconds the fire became so big! We didn't have any chance to get anything valuable in the house. Strangers came to help us by spraying water on the roof, to the trees, and all over the lawn. Our neighbor across the street on Coconut Street said that they called 911. Thanks for their alertness. My wife and I, being in the state of shock, cannot do anything except to pray to the Heavens for God to help us stop the fire. Before our eyes, the miracles started to happen.

In a short time, the fire trucks came roaring on Andrew Street with brave and courageous men in it. You all now have total control of the raging fire. We asked God to give you strength and protection for your safety. How could we ever thank you for saving our house from fire? If we cannot thank you enough, God will in our behalf. Along with this letter is a picture that I took after the fire. Again, thank you all very much for the bravery you have shown. Congratulations! And God bless...

Very truly yours,
Frank & Mary Grace De La Rosa

A timeless message exerpted from Pope Francis in one of his homilies:

"Many appreciate you, admire you and love you. Remember that to be happy is not to have a sky without a storm, a road without accidents, work without fatigue, relationships without disappointments. To be happy is to find strength in forgiveness, hope in battles, security in the stage of fear, love in discord. It is not only to enjoy the smile, but also to reflect on the sadness. It is not only to celebrate the successes, but to learn lessons from the failures. It is not only to feel happy with the applause, but to be happy in anonymity. Being happy is not a fatality of destiny, but an achievement for those who can travel within themselves. To be happy is to stop feeling like a victim and become your destiny's author. It is to cross deserts, yet to be able to find an oasis in the depths of our soul. It is to thank God for evely morning, for the miracle of life. Being happy is not being afraid of your own feelings. It's to be able to talk about you. It is having the courage to hear a "no". It is confidence in the face of criticism, even when unjustified. It is to kiss your children, pamper your parents, to live poetic moments with friends, even when they hurt us. To be happy is to let live the creature that lives in each of us, free, joyful and simple. It is to have maturity to be able to say: "I made mistakes". It is to have the courage to say "I am sorry". It is to have the sensitivity to say, "I need you". It is to have the ability to say "I love you". May your life become a garden of opportunities for happiness ... That in spring may it be a lover of joy. In winter a lover of wisdom. And when you make a mistake, start all over again. For only then will you be in love with life. You will find that to be happy is not to have a perfect life. But use the tears to irrigate tolerance. Use your losses to train patience. Use your mistakes to sculpt serenity. Use pain to plaster pleasure. Use obstacles to open windows of intelligence. Never give up .... Never give up on people who love you. Never give up on happiness, for life is an incredible show." -Pope Francis

The Rose Within

A certain man planted a rose and watered it faithfully and before it blossomed, he examined it. He saw the bud that would soon blossom, but noticed thorns upon the stem and he thought, "How can any beautiful flower come from a plant burdened with so many sharp thorns?" Saddened by the thought, he neglected to water the rose, and just before it was ready to bloom...it died.

So it is with many people. Within every soul there is a rose. The God-like qualities planted in us at birth, grow amid the thorns of our faults. Many of us look at ourselves and only see the thorns, the defects. We despair, thinking that nothing good can possibly comes from us. We neglect to water the good within us, and eventually it dies. We never realize our potential.

Some people do not see the rose within themselves; someone else must show it to them. One of the greatest gifts a person can possess is to be able to reach past the thorns of another, and find the rose within them. This is one of the greatest characteristics of love...to look at a person, know the true faults and accepting that person into your life...all the while recognizing the nobility in the soul. Help others to realize they can overcome their faults. If we show them the "rose" within themselves, they will conquer their thorns. Only then they will blossom many times over.

HOW TO STAY YOUNG

HOW TO STAY YOUNG

1. Throw out nonessential numbers. This includes age, weight and height. Let the doctors worry about them. That's why you pay them.
2. Keep only cheerful friends. The grouches pull you down.
3. Enjoy the simple things.
4. Laugh often, long and loud. Laugh until you gasp for breath.
5. The tears happen. Endure, grieve, and move on. The only person, who is with us our entire life, is ourselves.
6. Surround yourself with what you love, whether it's a family, pets, keepsakes, music, plants, hobbies, whatever. Your home is your refuge.
7. Cherish your health: If it is good, preserve it. If it is unstable, improve it. If it is beyond what you can improve, get help.
8. Look for a lovely thing, it's never far away. Marvel the wonders of God's creations all around you.
9. Tell people you love that you love them, at every opportunity.
10. Be at peace with yourself and above all with your God, whatever you conceive Him to be.

Psalm 23

The LORD is my shepherd; I shall not want.
He maketh me to lie down in green pastures:
He leadeth me beside the still waters.
He restoreth my soul:
He leadeth me in the paths of righteousness for his name's sake.
O, yeah, through I walk through the valley of the shadow of death,
I will fear no evil: For thou art with me;
Thy rod and thy staff they comfort me.
Thou preparest a table before me in the presence of mine enemies:
Thou anointest my head with oil; my cup runneth over.
Surely goodness and mercy shall follow me all the days of my life:
And I will dwell in the house of the LORD forever.

A PSALM OF LIFE

By Henry Wadsworth Longfellow
Tell me not in mournful numbers,
　Life is but an empty dream!
For the soul is dead that slumbers,
　And things are not what they seem.

Life is real! Life is earnest!
　And the grave is not its goal;
Dust thou are, to dust thou returnest,
　Was not spoken of the soul.

Not enjoyment, and not sorrow,
　Is our destined end or way;
But to act, that each tomorrow
　Find us farther than today.

Art is long, and Time is fleeting,
　And our hearts, though stout and brave,
Still, like muffled drums, are beating
　Funeral marches to the grave.

In the world's broad field of battle,
　In the bivouac of Life,
Be not like dumb, driven cattle!
　Be a hero in the strife!

Trust no Future, howe'er pleasant!
　Let the dead Past bury its dead!
Act, - act in the living Present!
　Heart within, and God o'erhead!

Lives of great men all remind us
　We can make our lives sublime,
And, departing, leave behind us
　Footprints on the sand of time;

Footprints, that perhaps another,
　Sailing o'er life's solenm main,
A forlorn and shipwrecked brother,
　Seeing, shall take heart again.

Let us then be up and doing,
　With a heart for any fate;
Still achieving, still pursuing,
　Learn to labor and to wait.

Panaguican Hill

by Frank A. De La Rosa

Still remember Panaguican Hill my old classmates dear?
In spite of our old age I hope you won't forget
The four-year of fond memories we had together
At the foot of that beautiful Panaguican Hill.

The Panaguican Hill was our eyes and ears
When working in the fishpond with nothing but shorts
From morning till noon we worked so hard
And back to the classroom to open up our books.

The work in the fishpond was hard and back-breaking
The mud was heavy and the muscles were small
But the shadows of the tall and swaying coconut palms
Gave us shade to make us cool from the heat of the sun.

Down and up the hill we go
The higher we go up, the better the view
Applied to life, we learned a lesson
That the higher we achieved the better we know.

I can never forget the incident that happened
While working in the fishpond alongside the foot of the hill
Under the supervision of our instructor who returned to the office
And came back scratching his head, to see no student we around.

The students hid in the bushes of Panaguican Hill
Burst into laughter when the instructor had no more students in view
However, with a little bit of luck, our beloved principal forgave us
Who understood what youthful indiscretion was all about.

Even though I live in a far away land
I kept all my fond memories in my heart
All the hardships, the sacrifices, and the struggles
At the foot of Panaguican Hill.

Note: This poem appeared in my book, A Touch of Life, page #108, and also in our Souvenir Program, Golden Jubilee Celebration, CAIC Class '58 Reunion, held in Panganiban, Catanduanes, on March 23, 24, and 25, 2008.

Philippine National Anthem

Land of the morning
Child of the sun returning
With fervor burning
Thee do our souls adore.
Land dear and holy,
Cradle of noble heroes,
Ne'er shall invaders
Trample thy sacred shores.
Ever within thy skies and through thy clouds
And o'er thy hills and seas;
Do we behold thy radiance, feel the throb
Of glorious liberty.
Thy banner dear to all hearts
Its sun and stars alright,
Oh, never shall its shining fields
Be dimmed by tyrants might.
Beautiful land of love, oh land of light,
In thine embrace 'tis rapture to lie;
But it is glory ever when thou art wronged
For us thy sons to suffer and die.

(English version)

PAMBANSANG AWIT NG PILIPINAS

Bayang magiliw
Perlas ng silanganan
Alab ng puso
Sa dibdib mo'y buhay
Lupang hinirang
Duyan ka ng magiting
Sa manlulupig
Di ka pasisiil
Sa dagat at bundok
Sa simoy at sa langit mong bughaw
May dilag ang tula
At awit sa paglayang minamhal
Ang kislap ng watawat mo'y
Tagumpay na nagniningning
Ang bituin at araw niya
Kailan pa ma'y di magdididlim
Lupa ng araw
Ng luwalhati't pagsinta
Buhay ay langit sa piling mo
Aming ligaya napag may mangaapi
Ay mamatay ng dahil saiyo.
(Tagalog version)

BAYAN KO

Ang bayan kong Pilipinas
Lupain ng ginto't bulaklak
Pag-ibig na sa kanyang palad
Nag-alay ng ganda't dilag
At sa kanyang yumi at ganda
Dayuhan ay nahalina
Bayan ko, binihag ka
Nasadlak sa dusa

Ibon mang may layang lumipad
Kulungin mo at umiiyak
Bayan pa kayang sakdal-dilag
Ang 'di magnasang makaalpas
Pilipinas kong minumutya
Pugad ng luha at dalita
Aking adhika
Makita kang sakdal laya.
(My Country)

A Time For Everything...

For everything there is a season,
a time for every activity under heaven.
A time to be born and a time to die.
A time to plant and a time to harvest.
A time to kill and a time to heal.
A time to tear down and a time build up.
A time to cry and a time to laugh.
A time to grieve and a time to dance.
A time to scatter stones and a time to gather stones.
A time to embrace and a time to turn away.
A time to search and a time to quit searching.
A time to keep and a time to throw away.
A time to tear and a time to mend.
A time to be quiet and a time to speak.
A time to love and a time to hate.
A time for war and a time for peace.
What do people really get for all their hard work?
I have seen the burden God has placed on us all.
Yet God has made everything beautiful for its own time.
He has planned eternity in the human heart, but even so,
people cannot see the whole scope of God's work
from beginning to end.

-Ecclesiastes 3

www.ingramcontent.com/pod-product-compliance
Lightning Source LLC
Chambersburg PA
CBHW060409010526
44107CB00005B/636